A Place in the Family:

Being a Single Person in the Local Church

by
David Gillett

In 1981 Member of Christian Renewal Centre, Rostrevor, N. Ireland
Since 1982 Vicar of St. Hugh's, Lewsey, Luton

and

Anne Long

In 1981 Tutor in Pastoral Counselling, St. John's College, Nottingham
Since 1985 working for Acorn Trust in the ministry of healing

and

Ruth Fowke

Consultant Psychiatrist, South West Surrey

GROVE BOOKS LIMITED
Bramcote   Nottingham   NG9 3DS

CONTENTS

Copyright David Gillett, Anne Long and Ruth Fowke 1981 and 1987

THE COVER PICTURE

is by Peter Ashton

NOTE TO SECOND EDITION

Although two of the three contributors are now in different ministries from those they were exercising when their chapters were first written, this second edition is published with only tiny corrections from the text of the original.

First Edition May 1981
Reprinted in Grove Books Limited Edition March 1987

ISSN 0144-171X
ISBN 1 85174 047 3

FOREWORD

This booklet began its life at a weekend houseparty for some of the single members of a local church. It became clear to the three of us how little understanding there was amongst both singles and marrieds within the church of the biblical teaching on singleness and how very little attention was given to the distinctive contributions as well as to the particular problems that single people have within the local congregation.

We are writing mainly about those who face the possibility of being single for life, though the issues raised are of importance for all people whether married or single. Shortage of space prevents us dealing with the particular problems faced by young people waiting for the right partner to come along, widows, divorcees or one parent families.

There is so little positive writing on this subject. For instance the note on celibacy in *Anglican Worship Today* (p189), which comes from the same 'Grove Books stable' as this booklet, explains that 'the new services do not provide for any "consecration" of celibacy, and in most cases celibacy is simply the condition of not having found the right marriage partner—yet'.

We write as those who are seeking to live as single people in the very different situations in which God has placed us—in 1981, a clergyman in an ecumenical Christian community, a member of staff in a Christian vocational college, and a doctor in a large local church. Our hope is that this booklet will help both those who are single, and those who are married, to be aware of the riches as well as the problems of being a Christian congregation made up of singles and couples.

SUGGESTED READING

Andrews, Gini	*Your Half of the Apple* (SLT Books, 1972).
Burrows, Ruth	*Guidelines in Mystical Prayer* (Sheed and Ward) 1976).
Clarkson, Margaret	*Single* (Kingsway, 1980).
Davidson,Alex	*The Returns of Love* (IVP, 1973).
Evening, Margaret	*Who Walk Alone* (Hodder and Stoughton, 1974).
Goergen, Donald	*The Sexual Celibate* (SPCK, 1976).
Hurding, Roger	*Restoring the Image* (Paternoster, 1980).
Lewis, C. S.	*The Four Loves* (Fontana, 1963).
Lum, Ada	*Single and Human* (IVP).
Nouwen, Henri	*Reaching Out* (Collins, 1976).
Powell, John	*Why am I afraid to Love?* (Fontana)
Trobisch, Walter	*Love Yourself* (IVP, 1976).
White, John	*Eros Defiled* (IVP, 1978).

1. THE BIBLICAL FOUNDATIONS

Many of the problems which single people experience stem from a lack of biblical teaching on this subject within the local church. Where such teaching is absent or only sketchily understood some may find themselves pressurized into a marriage which is outside the will of God for them (because they have no confidence from his word that God could well be calling them to singleness); yet others, who are single, might go through life condemned to feeling second-class citizens who have somehow 'missed out'—and all because of wrong attitudes based on the absence of a clear biblical understanding within their congregation.

1. Man, created as a sexual being

Perhaps the major theological problem surrounding singleness is the tendency to see celibacy almost exclusively in negative terms—the absence of marriage and the denial of sexuality. This negative view is in itself based on the false premise held by many throughout the Christian era, that sexuality is in some sense a shameful thing, almost the source of original sin. St. Ambrose typified this approach when he declared that 'married people ought to blush when they consider the kind of life they live.'

Consequently, both virginity and celibacy have been seen as the way of avoiding the contamination of sexual intercourse. In the case of the most celebrated virgin of all, the doctrine of the Perpetual Virginity evolved in part to preserve the absolute and life-long purity of the blessed Virgin Mary. Thus celibacy has been seen as the better way, for it is the more holy way. People who are married and who think blibically will rightly react against such a basis for singleness. Max Thurian, himself a celibate Taizé monastic brother similarly rejects this view. 'The Christian celibate has not given up sexual love in order to judge it impure. He knows its fulness and its demands. He is a normal human being. Having a full knowledge of the situation, he does not despise sexual life or make a false ideal of virginity for himself. In order to belong wholly to God without division, in service and in prayer, the Christian celibate has made the sacrifice of marital love for the sake of a great love for all men, the love of Christ which will fill all in everlasting life.'[1]

For some years there was another view of celibacy prevalent in some 'middle-class evangelical' circles. It was said that courtship and marriage tended to diminish the effectiveness of the young man's witness, so that when a Christian gets married he either becomes twice as effective for Christ or half as effective—and the strong implication often given was that the latter was more likely to happen than the former! This view—a kind of Bible-class version of monasticism—which can all too easily breed spiritual élitism has inevitably faded in popularity in the last two decades.

The rejection of these false bases for celibacy has the effect, especially among Protestants, of leaving marriage as the only state of life which has a consistently argued and generally accepted biblical basis. Consequently, there is often a real bias in Protestantism against any fully wholesome view of celibacy (all justification for it is somehow seen as discredited as springing from 'medieval' Roman Catholic ideas).

[1] *Marriage and Celibacy* (SCM, 1959) p.122.

Any view of celibacy which is to provide an adequate foundation for life cannot be based on spiritual èlitism or on any suggestion that sexuality and personal relationships are somehow unholy. Any who are encouraged to enter into a commitment to singleness on this basis are likely to find their vocation a crippling and unwholesome experience. Perhaps one of the greatest dangers for single people is that they approach their life feeling they have said goodbye to certain things in their makeup which, in truth, can never be dismissed and without which no human being can grow healthily to maturity. In fact, the biblical starting point for both marriage and celibacy is identical: man is a sexual being who accepts the goodness of his own sexuality and values deeply the richness of human relationships.

The creation narrative in Genesis 2 provides two clear declarations which are basic to the wholeness of every human being—married or single. *Man is made for fellowship.* After the creation of Adam we are told of the divine discontent with man: 'It is not good that man should be alone' (Gen.2.18). In order to experience and grow into the fulness of what it means to be human, man must live in fully satisfying relationship with other people, and this relationship is seen supremely in marriage (Gen. 2.18-24). 'It is fundamental to this need in man that relationships should be both reciprocal and free. Adam therefore rejects as inadequate all the animals that were brought before him: none of them can be a 'helper fit for him'. Man was placed by God before a choice and decision which he was consciously to make and verbally confess. Not only was he to receive his partner or helpmeet, but he was to discover the helpmeet as such and freely to accept her. She was to become to him in his own recognition what she really is, and to be acknowledged and welcomed as such by his own free word. The recognition of the I in the THOU.[1] Adam's "Eureka" expresses his confidence that he will realize his full humanity in relationship with Eve—'This at last is bone of my bones and flesh of my flesh' (Gen. 2.23).

If Karl Barth is right, and I believe he is, then the absolute centrality of 'relationship' in man's essential make-up is also evident in the teaching of Genesis 1. The meaning of 'man made in the image of God' which the text itself suggests is that of a personality who, like God, exists in mutual relationship. For God, though one, is not solitary ('let *us* make man in *our* image'—Gen. 1.26). The phrase 'male and female he created them' also stands alongside the declaration that man is made in the image of God (Gen. 1.27). Thus, the clearest expression of man being in the image of God is to be seen in the depth, and the mutual relationship that is possible within marriage. It is from this fundamental truth of human existence that all else flows. It is because man is capable of such relationships that he can converse with God, and thus govern creation on God's behalf.

Genesis 2 also declares that *sexuality is a good gift from God.* The final verdict is that 'man and his wife were both naked and not ashamed' (Gen. 2.25). It follows from these two declarations that any person, married or single, who seeks to live in isolation and refuses to accept his sexuality is building on an inherently inadequate foundation. If a successful marriage depends largely on how a couple grow in their special relationship within the wider social context of other relationships which make up their life and

1 Karl Barth *Church Dogmatics* III (T. and T. Clark, 1975) p. 292.

how they accept, complement, and satisfy one another sexually, so also a full single life depends on the openness and growth in relationships with others, and a positive acknowledgement and acceptance of one's sexuality. The single life is sometimes lived as a solitary existence devoid of relationship and one where all awareness of sexuality is rejected or, at the most, kept quiet as a guilty secret. When that is true, either by design or default, life is severely impoverished and growth inevitably stunted.

Both of these truths are now to be seen from the perspective of our fallenness. Some single people make life difficult for themselves by viewing marriage in all the idealism of Genesis 2 while themselves living as single persons experiencing the full effects of the fall described in Genesis 3. But, just as the basic truths of man's created nature apply consistently to both celibate and married, so the effects of the fall apply to both singles and couples alike. Relationships now experience tyranny (Gen. 3.16) and sexuality is now surrounded by the shame brought in by rebellion, pride and greed (Gen. 3.7,10). Therefore, the single person who believes that his problem of loneliness would immediately and conclusively be solved by marriage, is deluded. He needs to remember that marriages experience the same effects of fallenness with which he is grappling and that there are, for instance, many marriages where there is so little experience of relationship left that the partners know loneliness at its most acute.

There can never, in this age, be a return to the paradisiacal experiences of the perfect relationship[1] and the completely unsullied experience of sexuality described in Genesis 2. The story itself shows God acknowledging this fact by making clothes for Adam and Eve (Gen. 3.21) and guarding the pre-fall experience with the heavenly sentry (Gen. 3.24). Any 'back-to-nature' theories fail to acknowledge the radical truth of Genesis 3. 'The preservation of shame in the fallen world is the only—although a most contradictory—possibility of acknowledging the original nakedness and blessedness of the nakedness. This is not because shame itself is something good in itself—that is the moralistic, puritanical, totally unbiblical interpretation—but because it must give reluctant witness to its own fallen state.'[2]

The only true basis for the single life is an acknowledgement of the nature of man as a sexual being who needs loving relationships, and an awareness that the problems encountered in that calling should not be seen primarily as the natural results of not being married, but as the inevitable consequences of being part of fallen humanity.

2. The call of Jesus to singleness

It is clear from the creation narratives that God's intention is that man's sexuality and need for reciprocal relationship will be found in marriage. Thus the logical climax of the creation story is that 'man leaves his father and mother and cleaves to his wife and they become one flesh' (Gen. 2.24). Thus, throughout the Old Testament, and right until the time of Jesus, the calling of God to everyone was seen in terms of marriage.

It is because many Christians today consider this teaching to be the total Christian view that singleness is often seen as a negative concept. It is

1 See *A Severe Mercy* by Vanauken (Hodder and Stoughton, 1977), for a moving account of the attempt and failure to find a firm basis of life in the perfect relationship.
2 Bonhoeffer *Creation and Fall* (London, 1966) p.80.

basically problematic in a way that marriage is not. But such a view stems from a failure to perceive the truly revolutionary change brought about by the life and teaching of Jesus. Celibacy, for the followers of the Messiah, becomes a state into which they can be called as an integral part of their discipleship. In the fulness of the kingdom of God, says Jesus, there will be no marrying (Matt. 22.30), and, as this kingdom is experienced within by the followers of Christ in this present age, some will live in that state determined by God's original creation, but others in that anticipated by the presence of the kingdom of God here and now. For the Christian this brings a fundamental change in how he views the possibility of life. For him both marriage and celibacy are normal possibilities, though one has been possible from the beginning of God's creation, and the other since the coming of the kingdom of Christ.

Jesus makes this position clear in his discussion with the disciples which follows his teaching on divorce in Matthew 19.10-12. 'The disciples said to him, "If such is the case of a man with his wife, it is not expedient to marry." But he said to them, "Not all men can receive this precept, but only those to whom it is given. For there are eunuchs who have been so from birth, and there are eunuchs who have been made eunuchs by men, and there are eunuchs who have made themselves eunuchs for the sake of the kingdom of heaven. He who is able to receive this, let him receive it".' The disciples are obviously overwhelmed by the demands of Jesus' teaching on the nature of marriage and feel that it might be easier not to marry at all. Jesus takes up this statement by giving clear teaching on the possibility of remaining single and foregoing sexual intercourse for life.

According to this teaching, the unmarried life is possible only for three classes of people. There are those who are incapable of sexual intercourse because of some physical incapacity with which they were born. There are others who have been castrated for some reason which Jesus does not specify. Though the practice is quite alien to modern western culture, many societies have practised castration for those serving in royal palaces, particularly within the harem. Some priests in pagan temples, for instance those who served in the temple of Diana in Ephesus, were also made eunuchs. Moreover, some ascetic sects, like the Essenes, practised castration. Then thirdly, there are those who voluntarily forego the possibility of sexual intercourse for life for the sake of the kingdom of God. But no one is to choose the celibate life for himself.[1] It is for those 'to whom it is given' as a gift from God. If, says Jesus, a man is able to receive this, if, that is, he finds the grace of God within him, enabling him to respond to this call, then he should accept it as God's way for him to live within the kingdom of God. Jesus clearly regards both marriage and celibacy as difficult and demanding—both are to be seen as part of the radical call to forsake the ways of the world, to follow him and to live as heirs of the kingdom. 'The important thing is not whether I am celibate or married: it is whether I am living in expectation of God's coming kingdom'.[2]

1 On the basis of this teaching of Jesus some include various categories of emotional wounding which renders one incapable of a successful marriage. Developed in this way the text has obvious relevance to the question of homosexuality.
2 Donald Goergen *The Sexual Celibate* (SPCK, 1976) p.27.

3. St. Paul's teaching on sexuality and singleness

St. Paul develops Jesus' teaching and clearly sees celibacy as one of the two options for all Christians. From 1 Corinthians 7 it would appear that Paul had been asked what was the Christian teaching on remaining celibate for life. In the Greek world there was considerable admiration for celibacy and other ascetic practices. Perhaps members of the Corinthian Church wished to adopt this as part of the Christian pattern of living.[1] Also at the back of Paul's mind were the various reports which he had received about fornication and adultery within the Church of Corinth. He is thus dealing with two extremes: the 'ascetics' who held that marriage was dangerous and polluting and the 'enlightened party' who saw celibacy as totally unnecessary and contemptible. To the former he says, 'The husband should give to his wife her conjugal rights, and likewise the wife to her husband' (v3). To the latter he says that celibacy is indeed an acceptable calling (v1) and one in which he himself glories (v7). The opening two verses of the chapter could be paraphrased in this way. 'You asked me if you should remain unmarried as a Christian. Well, it is certainly a most acceptable calling for a Christian. It is certainly a possibility that God would have you remain single (I'll tell you the reasons later). But it is no easy thing to remain single, and it's even more difficult in Corinth where you are surrounded by sexual immorality on every side. Therefore, it is probably best, in the first instance, that you should look to marriage as your calling'. Paul opens by dampening their enthusiasm for celibacy, and it is only later, after writing of the positive duties of man and wife, that he gives his own testimony on the matter. He cannot imagine any other state giving such happiness, so completely fulfilled is he in his own celibacy, yet he is quite clear that 'each has his own special gift from God, one of one kind and one of another' (v7b). Celibacy is thus a 'charisma', one of the gifts of the Spirit, given by God to some members of the Body of Christ so that they can remain single and enjoy it. As with all 'charismata' this gift is given for the benefit of the whole body (1 Cor. 7.7), and thus men and women who are celibate are part of God's plan for his people and they should be accepted and honoured as such. The distinctive nature of the gift of celibacy from which the whole body benefits is that the single person is 'free from anxieties' (amerimnos—v32). Marrieds have the cares of looking after partners and families but those who have the charisma of singleness do not have the same ties and can give their whole energies to the work of Christ's body, and this is especially important in the troubled times which Paul sees coming upon the Church as the return of Christ draws near (vv 26 and 29). No spiritual gift should be a cause of pride in those who possess it and neither should it be coveted on the one hand nor despised on the other by those who do not have that particular gift.[2]

4. Jesus, a model of fulfilled celibacy

In Jesus' life we see the clearest example of what it means to remain single for the sake of the kingdom. He demonstrates how to live as a single person

[1] Such ascetic tendenceis are clearly denounced as false teaching which fails to receive with thanksgiving God's good gifts (1 Tim. 4.1-5).

[2] The teaching of the New Testament does not deal directly with two very important areas of singleness as we know it today, i.e. those who feel a short term call to celibacy and those who are single because they have not been able to find a suitable Christian partner. These issues are dealt with in the second section of this booklet.

while knowing fulfilment in the two basic areas highlighted in the creation narratives. He lives in deep and meaningful relationships with others and shows all the signs of openly accepting his own sexuality. As in Adam, the first man of creation, we discover the perfection of marriage, so in Christ, the second Adam and the first man of the kingdom we are confronted with the perfection of singleness.

Jesus, though called to a ministry which, in the end, could only be fulfilled in total aloneness, lives closely in relationship with other people. His relationships with his own disciples are very important to him—in the Garden of Gethsemane he seems to count a lot on their presence and understanding (Mark 14.32-42). There is the smaller group of Peter, James and John (Mark 9.2, 14.33) in whom he seems to confide at a deeper level than with the rest of the twelve, and, with the one whom we know as 'the beloved disciple' (John 19.26 etc.), probably John, the son of Zebedee, he has a particularly close relationship.

He regards these disciples as 'family'. His own childhood within the family at Nazareth had been a model of dependence, growth and security (Luke 2.51-52). He would know the importance of family and early on he perceived the true nature of that family into which all need to grow as they contemplate the necessity of leaving the childhood home. After his visit to the Temple as a twelve-year-old Mary finds him and asks him, 'Son, why have you treated us so? Behold *your* father and I have been looking for you anxiously.' Mary is clearly thinking in terms of Jesus' security within his childhood family but Jesus himself has already perceived that new experience of family in which he would find his meaning and security as an adult—'How is it that you sought me? Did you not know that I must by in *my* Father's house?' (Luke 2.48-49). It is in this context that Jesus finds all the resources of family life which provide the environment for fulfilling relationships which is a constant need for healthy development throughout the whole of life. Thus, when Jesus is told that Mary and some of his family are outside, he asks 'Who are my mother and my brothers?' And looking around on those who sat about him, he said, 'Here are my mother and my brothers.' Whoever does the will of God is my brother and sister and mother' (Mark 3.32-35). Jesus recognizes the continuing need for relationships that fulfil parental roles (of caring, wisdom, dependability etc.), the brotherly roles (of sharing, discovery, play etc.) and the feminine 'homely' roles (see his warm relationships with women). For a child these are provided in the trusting environment of the family home, as an adult these are found in the similar environment of the family of God, where one belongs, and is accepted without question and where recognition is not something that has to be fought for—it is just there! Central in this new family is the relationship with the Father. In the Garden of Gethsemane only eleven of his closest brothers are with him; he takes three with him to watch and pray: but, at such a critical time, it is with the Father alone that he shares fellowship (Mark 14.32-42).

As all humans are born into a family, all need the close, secure, dependable relationships of the family throughout the whole of life. Yet it is important that a man or woman should leave the parental home (Gen. 2.24). In the created order this leads inevitably to marriage, to the creating of another family environment in which the couple continue to grow. The kingdom of God brings a new possibility. Jesus shows that 'growing-up' involves leaving the parental home in order to enter into the ongoing family experience of God's people. The richness and naturalness of familial relationships continue to be important throughout life and consequently the single person who is called to live according to the reality of the kingdom of God where there is no marriage will only find that security and growth that he needs if the church is actually living in the kingdom reality of the family of God. It is because single people so often have to live out their kingdom-calling in a church which is living in the old order that their lives so easily become cold, lonely, and stunted.

But for Jesus, the kingdom experience of family was a present reality in which he also showed an open acceptance of his sexuality. Sexual intercourse was never his experience—sexual relationships, both heterosexual and homosexual being against the will of God for single people.[1] His whole life shows how false is the prevalent opinion that no man can live a full life without genital experience.[2] He shows the open acceptance of his sexuality in the affective side of his nature—he freely shows gentleness, compassion, warmth, and love, he is not afraid of touch and physical contact as a means of interpersonal communication, he is openly receptive to young children, he weeps in public and is unembarrassed by it, and he accepts generously the extravagance of love offered by Mary Magdalene.

In short, Jesus demonstrates the naturalness with which sexuality affects the life of the single person with all the richness it brings to his personality, relationships and emotional life. The problems of loneliness and genitality which single people often feel so acutely are not so much due to their state (assuming that is indeed God's call and gift to them) but to the lack of a truly kingdom-style environment. Wherever the church fails to be the family of God where all types of familial relationships are freely and naturally present, singleness is bound to be a problem. It can make it near-impossible for a single person to know whether he is called to celibacy—he knows he experiences loneliness and frustration, but is this because he is not called to singleness or because the church is not the family of God as it ought to be? If he becomes convinced that celibacy is his call he knows he has to live out this kingdom-call in a non-kingdom-like environment. If we are to be biblical and encourage individuals to accept God's call to singleness (the alternative is yet more marriages outside of God's will) then the local church must be careful that it is responding to the call of the kingdom to be, in reality, the family of God.

---

[1] See Gen. 2.23-25, Deut. 22.13-20, 1 Cor. 7.1-9, and Gen. 19.1-11, Lev. 18.22, Rom. 1.18-23.

[2] So much of the approach of the Gay Christian Movement is based on the assumption that man must inevitably fulfil his genital urges or forever remain deprived and stunted. Jesus shows the lie to this near-universal belief of our age.

2. TOWARDS A POSITIVE VIEW OF SINGLENESS

1. Different attitudes to singleness

It is all too easy to jump to false conclusions about how single people feel.

'She *must* be frustrated—*forty* and not married!'
'He's such a nice fellow—I wonder why he's not married yet?'

Or, at the other extreme,

'With a good career and a beautiful home, she doesn't *need* a husband'
'He's doing such strategic work for God—it would be a *waste* for him to marry'

Such statements presuppose all kinds of questionable attitudes, both in those who make them and in those talked about. Most single people find themselves moving through different phases of hoping, enjoying, hurting, longing, rejecting and accepting at different stages of their lives.

(a) Most young people will be hoping for marriage and living in the expectation that they will, one day, marry and have a family. And this is a right and good expectation, though the challenge (and sometimes the pinch) is to live in the present rather than the future, using one's energies for God and his kingdom.

(b) The years tick by—for some very happily—until a man or woman in, say, late twenties or thirties may be feeling more keenly about marriage. Perhaps, beneath a positive exterior, doubts and questions loom—

'Am I attractive to the opposite sex?'
'Am I normal?'
'I'm on the shelf'
'I've never even been asked'

Sometimes insensitive jokes (often at friends' weddings) accentuate discomfort and increase loneliness—

'Never say die!'
'It might be your turn next'
'Good things come to those who wait!'

But again, the challenge is to live in the present rather than in day-dreams, and to hold on to the truth, however hard, that God has a plan for each person that is good and creative, as well as resources to fulfil that plan. It can help to have honest discussion with other singles, and marrieds too, about one's singleness.

(c) By the time a single person has reached his or her forties, there may still be a deep longing for marriage, but diminishing hopes. It is wonderful to have nine god-children (as I have!) but there is also the fact that a woman is increasingly unlikely to conceive and bear her own children. Also marriage is far less likely now, unless it be to a widower or widow. The greatest dangers at this stage are self-centredness and resentment. Moreover, these very things can make one far less attractive to the opposite sex! It is far more difficult for a busy mother to become self-centred than for a single person. It is all too easy to let one's use of time, gifts, recreation and choice revolve around one's own preferences and aversions. And, if they go unchecked, hurts and grievances can quickly develop into resents, blaming God, others and oneself. It is one thing to know that there are more women than men in the church, but it is another to realize that you are one of those women who won't marry! Here again, sharing with others can help, and where we can not only share but minister mutually, then the aches and resents can be released and healed to become places of understanding for others.

(d) What about the single person who begins to think his or her state might be God's choice and calling? This does not mean that the flesh no longer tugs towards a partner. Rather, there will come the growing awareness of invitation not to loss but to finding a calling which *includes* one's singleness. Such an invitation does not by-pass one's sexuality, rather, it requires it. It will not be 'second best' but a calling chosen for one by God.

(e) Some who are exploring singleness as a possible calling, may want to make a short-term commitment to celibacy. It is not only in monasteries where this can happen! Some modern Christian communities are experimenting with such commitment, as also are individuals living outside a community setting. It might be something known only to God and the person involved, or it might be something talked and prayed through with a church leader. The advantage is that for a given period (e.g. one year) one lives *within* that commitment and channels one's energies accordingly. If God gives the good gift of marriage, then the commitment will terminate after the agreed time.

(f) For some, singleness can and will become a positive and lasting vocation. And such a calling, whilst not depending on a declaration of commitment, might be strengthened by making one, alone before God or with a Christian leader present. If this is to happen, it will certainly not be through a denial of one's sexuality. An offering of what is semi-repressed or denied is hardly an offering. We rightly suspect that pietism which is escapist and other-worldly, shocked by body and earthiness. Simon Tugwell O.P. said that 'celibacy must be witness to a fully human mode of life which does not need or fear idols. As long as the celibate is on the run from sexuality, (s)he is still offering it worship. (S)he must be undaunted by it, willing to form rich human relationships without fear of affection, without fear of bodiliness'. We shall come back to this later.

2. Discovery of a positive attitude

Shut your eyes for a moment and answer this question—'What does personal fulfilment in relationships mean to me, whether I am married or single?'

The Bible's answer is neither marriage nor singleness, but life in Christ characterized by love. Such a life will be marked by a growing wholeness and maturity. Paul's pastoral goal was 'to present every man mature in Christ', to lead people to 'mature manhood'. This maturity reflects a growing 'shalom', or harmony at every level, and is quite independent of being married or single. Jim Punton describes 'shalom' as 'a totally integrated life of body, heart and mind, attuned to nature, open to others, in joy with

God, of sharing, mutuality and love; of justice, freedom, interdependence.'[1] Such wholeness is part of our salvation and does not imply marriage. One can, in Christ, be single and whole, and to think otherwise is to fall short of Biblical teaching. Growth in 'shalom' is for singles and marrieds alike. So the question of personal fulfilment will not hinge on marriage but on growth in wholeness. We can look at four related areas to clarify this— relationships, sexuality, lifestyle, and gifts.

a. *Maturing in relationships*
Relationship with God will include coming to know our unconditional acceptance by him, our resources in him, our obedience to him. The single person can discover an exciting growth in intimacy with God through prayer. When my married colleagues return to their families for tea, I often spend some 'lap-time' with God, simply being with him at that stage of the day.

Our human relationships should also be growing ones. Jesus' basis for his own relationships was not marriage but friendship—with both sexes, with marrieds, singles and children. Older people can provide resources of listening, praying, and supporting. Married friends strengthen family links— a married person often needs the friendship of a single one just as much as the other way round. A family can also be a wonderful way for growing friendships with children. I know a single woman who sometimes invites an eight-year-old boy (one of six children) for a Saturday. They go out together, cook, have treats and talk as real friends. Undoubtedly, children have their own unique ministry to single people.

Obviously there are dangers of insensitivity when a single person lives in the pocket of married friends, not realizing that husband and wife need their own times together. There can sometimes develop a lop-sided attachment to one of the partners. In an insecure marriage this can present hazards which are all too easy to rationalize. Many mistakes in loving have been made both by singles and marrieds. The answer lies not in ceasing to love but in seeking to discover appropriate loving. Margaret Evening writes:

'A love that is warm, tender and outgoing, that wants the highest and best for others, that is not afraid to express itself in all the legitimate ways open to it, a love which can stand the searchlight of God's holiness and not shrivel—that is the love that we must aim at and seek to make our ethic in every situation. That sort of love scarcely leaves room for any furtive relationship.'[2]

The single person needs friends of both sexes, and some friendships that are closer than others, The person who cannot sustain and deepen a few particular friendships is not maturing. But when does a special friendship lapse into the category of 'exclusive' or 'possessive' or 'inordinate'? C. S. Lewis writes:

'Lovers are always talking to one another about their love; Friends hardly ever talk about their Friendship. Lovers are normally face to face, absorbed in each other; Friends side by side, absorbed in some common interest.'[3]

---

1 Jim Punton *The Community of Shalom, God's Radical Alternative* (Frontier Youth Trust).
2 Margaret Evening *Who Walk Alone* (Hodder and Stoughton, 1974) p.104.
3 C. S. Lewis, *The Four Loves* (Fontana, 1963) p.73.

Friendship that becomes exclusive or possessive will soon—ironically—miss out on what true friendship is. Particularly if we feel needy for affection and closeness, we can want a friend for what we can get out of him. But loving another means allowing him his own autonomy and identity as a person. We have to love him for what he is in himself, not for the good we get out of him.

Where does homosexual relationship feature in our thinking about friendship? We cannot enter a full discussion here, but readers are recommended to read chapter 3 of Margaret Evening's *Who Walk Alone,* also Alex Davidson's *The Returns of Love.* Both writers plead for generosity of attitude to those who are homosexually orientated (and this can include marrieds as well as singles). Both also plead for discipline when it comes to homosexual practice.

To explore loving relationships of any kind is costly. Mistakes are inevitable; but perhaps the only ultimate mistake is to cease trying! To love anyone is to make yourself vulnerable. C. S. Lewis writes:

'If you want to make sure of keeping it intact, you must give your heart to no-one . . . lock it up safe in the casket or coffin of your selfishness. But in that casket—safe, dark, motionless, airless—it will change. It will not be broken; it will become unbreakable, impenetrable, irredeemable.

' . . . We shall draw nearer to God, not by trying to avoid the sufferings inherent in all loves, but by accepting them and offering them to Him; throwing away all defensive armour.'[1]

For some, however, there is the opposite and subtle danger of dealing with loneliness by over-sharing. Real openness to each other also means real closedness—not a furtive, exclusive attitude but one that preserves the uniqueness of the other person. Inappropriate over-sharing will not (paradoxically) meet the need for intimacy. Indeed, it can lead to a parasitic, sentimental relationship. Henri Nouwen writes:

'The mystery of love is that it protects and respects the aloneness of the other and creates the free space where he can convert his loneliness into a solitude that can be shared. In this solitude we can strengthen each other by mutual respect, by careful consideration of each other's individuality, by an obedient distance from each other's privacy and by a reverent understanding of the sacredness of the human heart . . . In this solitude we can slowly become aware of a presence of him who embraces friends and lovers and offers us the freedom to love each other, because he loved us first.'[2]

So aloneness can be converted into solitude, and here is a thought for marrieds as well as singles. Within the marriage relationship there is also a right nurture of solitude as well as togetherness, for at the end of the day each person must stand on his or her own before God. Many marrieds have never come to terms with solitude, and singles could well have a ministry to them here. As they begin to discover the good gift for themselves, so their sharing of it will not only safeguard the privacy of the other but also build him up.

[1] C. S. Lewis *The Four Loves* (Fontana, 1963) pp.138-9.
[2] Henri Nouwen *Reaching Out* (Collins, 1976) p.44.

The single person should also be seeking a growing harmony in himself. Hopefully he will be growing in his personal identity—that which makes him uniquely himself. 'Shalom', harmony at every level, can become a growing reality as spirit, mind, attitudes, emotions, behaviour, body, past and present become integrated into personal identity. Obviously this takes time. There is a self-nurture that is not selfish but part of maturing. Jesus told us 'love your neighbour as yourself', and there is a right as well as a wrong self-love. Some Christians ironically strive and strain to give up a self they have never found. No wonder the result can look inhuman!

b *Maturing in sexuality*

In section one we said that a full single life depends not only on growth in relationships but also on a positive acknowledgement and acceptance of the good gift of our sexuality. But what kind of 'good gift' is this that cannot be consummated?

Donald Goergen, in his book *The Sexual Celibate,* makes an interesting and persuasive distinction between sexuality and genitality. Genitality, he says, is only one dimension of our sexuality; there is also a social dimension, which he calls our affectivity. The genital dimension is primarily biological and physiological, whereas the affective dimension concerns the affectionate, compassionate, tender aspects of our sexuality, which need not be genital but can be socialized—though only as we confront and become comfortable with our own biological drives. As we become free to own and express our affection, compassion and tenderness, so we grow in our sexuality, despite not being free to use our genitality. This will lead us into many different expressions of caring, loving, praying, creative activity. We need to affirm our sexuality, accepting our bodies and emotions and genitality without fear of guilt, discovering our affectivity, tenderness, compassion, working out our masculinity and femininity in growing relationships.

Obviously, such growth will involve pain. Ruth Burrows writes:

'Being sexual basically means I am a half and not a whole; it means accepting the fact of incompleteness, and this incompleteness involves pain . . . This means having to face and cope with the pain of a raw surface for many a long year, until God fills up the spaces on every level and we become whole in Him.'[1]

What do we do with our genital instincts? Some find relief in masturbation and can accept this. But many feel guilty and keep it to themselves as a shameful secret. We can look at masturbation in two ways. Firstly, there is the sort that gives quick physical relief to pent-up sexual energy, and secondly, the sort accompanied by fantasy relationships with real or imagined people. There is no need for undue guilt over the first sort, but there is a need to live in reality. If masturbation becomes a substitute for real, growing relationships, it is likely to heighten loneliness and longing. Far better use one's energies to work at real relationships rather than fantasy ones and, where possible, to offer to God those genital drives whose energies might be more creatively channelled in other ways.

1 Ruth Burrows *Guidelines to Mystical Prayer* (Sheed and Ward, 1976) p.81.

I like these words of a celibate priest, 'We can't hope to attain to a practice of celibacy which is positive, unafraid, unembarrassed, fully bodily, fully emotional, frank and humanly integrated, simply by our own resources. Our confidence must be in God's grace . . . It is in Christ the Single One that we can hope to become single both in the sense of being unmarried and in the sense of being inwardly undivided.'

c. *Maturing in lifestyle*

One of Paul Tournier's books is called *A Place for You,* and in it he explores the idea that all of us need 'somewhere to be'. It might be a whole house or just one room, but it is important that, however limited, we have our own place which becomes an expression and extension of our own personality.

There are so many ways of being creative, and this does not necessarily require unlimited money. When I moved into my college teaching job with a college flat, I prayed hard that, with not much money to spend and next to no furniture, I would be able to create a home that I and others would enjoy. The answers to that prayer were more tasteful than I had feared! I was given things that were just right! Although I felt guilty about buying the pine table and chairs I had always wanted, I did, and have never regretted it. I have no garden, but a window box and house plants give pleasure. I'm not a brilliant cook, but occasional creative entertaining is very enjoyable, and I've picked up many tips from Edith Schaeffer's *Hidden Art* about the small touches that turn something ordinary into something special—a candle, a floating flower, etc.

A home is for enjoying, not only by others but by ourselves on our own. Loneliness can turn into quiet solitude. We need the courage to 'enter into the desert of our loneliness and change it by gentle and persistent efforts into a garden of solitude.'[1] This is not selfish, but part of our maturing as single people.

d. *Maturing in gifts*

Paul writes to the Romans that, as they have different gifts, they should use them. That may sound very obvious, but many people (and not only singles) find it hard to believe they have any gifts. Read Romans 12.6-8 and 1 Corinthians 12.4-11 and check which gifts you have. The range is wide—teaching, administration, giving, praying, encouragement, serving, etc. And these are only representative gifts. There are many others as well—music, carpentry, art, sewing, cooking, mechanical skills, decorating, visiting, etc.

Recently I met a single girl in her twenties. She is not strong physically yet has moved into a tower block flat in an urban overspill parish where vandalism abounds. She teaches physically handicapped children, was church organist, helped the music group, was on the P.C.C., organized missionary groups and Christian Aid Week, and she regularly had people (including children) home for meals. If we wanted a job done well, we could rely on her. What a gem!

1 Henri Nouwen, *Reaching Out* (Collins, 1976) p.35.

But church is not the only context for gifts. Evening classes, summer schools, special interest clubs can also be places of enrichment, friendship and fun. It is part of good stewardship to know how we are growing in the gifts we have, discovering new ones, and sharing them with others.

3. The Pros and Cons of singleness

There are many circumstances in life where the grass on the other side seems greener, and sighing for another patch is bound to increase discontent. Yet it is also realistic to admit to difficult areas.

For many, the greatest difficulty will be loneliness, whether experienced sexually, socially, or practically. To accept the reality of one's singleness won't necessarily remove the pangs, but by acknowledging them and holding them to God, the pain is more likely to turn into offering than resentment. In our bodies we were meant for complementarity and the body's clamour is natural. But, personally, I'd rather be reminded of my sexuality than never feel it!

We may feel the loneliness socially when we don't have a partner in company, or we may feel it over such practicalities as the car breaking down, a hole to be darned, Income Tax forms, accounts, etc. There are many more resources for helping oneself in such practicalities than there used to be. And such needs can also encourage us to reach out more often to friends and those whose skills we need.

A more serious disadvantage is a growing concentration upon self. It may show itself in fussiness, narrowness, inflexibility, etc. Hopefully our best friends will tell us when this begins to happen!

But what about the advantages of being single? The greatest, as I see it, are our freedoms. Many of us have considerable freedom in the use of our time. Many of us have freedom of movement. All of us have the freedom to exercise choice. Granted there are some whose devotion to others— especially parents—means they do not have unlimited freedom, especially at certain stages of life. Yet few people have the time-consuming commitments that a mother or father has. Lacking these commitments, they have more opportunity to explore certain areas of Christian ministry which might not be so open a choice for marrieds, such as inner city ministry or work overseas, where such considerations as children's education and the needs of a partner do not have to be borne in mind by singles.

Singleness can, if seen as such, become a wonderful gift from God which, in turn, we can return in offering to God for his chosen use. It will be a more costly vocation for some than for others, but as we explore its vocational possibilities so we shall discover its riches. Brother Roger of Taizé points us in the best direction when, out of his own vocation to singleness, he writes:

'Only when our eyes are fixed on Christ is the slow transformation possible. Gradually our natural human-love turns into a living Christ-love; we find ourselves on the far side of the difficulties. Our heart, our affections, our senses, our human nature are all present and fully alive, but with Another than ourselves transfiguring them!'

3. THE CHURCH AND SINGLE PEOPLE

In looking at the church as family, then at relationships, responsibility and recreation in that family, we cannot confine ourselves only to the place of single people. What is written here is not peculiar to singles, but is of particular relevance to them, and especially those without close natural ties.

1. The church as family

What does the phrase 'the church family' really mean? Too often the idea of a church family is limited to that of a family church, that is to say one that encourages existing families to do things (and especially to worship) together. Of course this is necessary, but there is much more to the concept of the church as family. The church family is so much more than an agreeable association of two generation families.

 How any given church regards itself can be portrayed visually, as these examples show. The drawing on the left is taken from a church letterhead adopted in 1978. Some months later another church in an adjoining county also designed a logo with a similarly stylized nuclear family, the parents sitting close together and a 'unisex' child standing by each, a symbol it is still using. Happily the first church has now progressed to using the drawing on the right— a small but significant difference.

a. *Enduring relationship*

The idea of family is surely that of people in a particular relationship to each other, an enduring relationship that adapts to the inevitable changes of growth and development in its members. When John is ten his constant companion is James, at fifteen he wants to be with the 'in' crowd of fellows and girls, but by eighteen he spends all his spare time with Jane. A healthy family adapts to these changes and is not broken or weakened by the constantly shifting pattern of inter-relatedness between its various members. It is the family which provides the living environment designed to encourage its various members to grow in a way that will help them develop all aspects of their God-given personality, and it continues to provide this essential security throughout all stages of their lives from birth to death. This calls for give-and-take on the part of all, which is not easy to sustain between those who have not chosen each other.

b. *As of right*

Every person needs a sense of belonging, of belonging to and being accepted by other people AS OF RIGHT. In the church family everyone matters. Being committed to one another as people, we care for each other in the small, mundane matters of daily life, sharing the humdrum aspects as well as the highlights. This mutual care and concern is a secure framework which provides a good foundation for further growth. Single people over thirty may need particular help to realize that they genuinely belong and have a place especially for *them* in the church precisely because our culture so emphasizes marriage, or at least living together.

c. *Despite contradictions*

A natural family behaves differently in different circumstances, and at varying stages in its own development. Parents and children sitting together in church, or playing in the local park, present a public picture quite different from some very private scenes behind their own closed front door. It is often said that home is where we're loved the most and behave the worst. For any church to BE family it must be able to tolerate the perplexing contradictions that unquestionably exist somewhere in everyone.

Denying the dark side of life does not make it go away. The church family founded by the love of Jesus and held together through his abundant grace and forgiveness, should afford its members the comfort of getting out of their psychological Sunday best and being able to be at ease with each other just as they are really are at the moment.

The church as family needs to be able to hold in harmony the tension between what is possible in Christ, and what each individual really is in stark reality. Christians need to be able to be open with each other, or at least with some others in the family, about their hopes and fears, successes and failures, dreams and doubts, without always having to live up to an idealized image of what 'a good Christian' ought to be.

d. *Ensuring privacy*

A warm and loving family minimizes the likelihood of its members being lonely but may not fully appreciate the need for individuals to have a measure of solitude as well as company. People can only grow as people when they have a relationship with others and with themselves, and it is this latter relationship that is so often avoided. We fill our days with activity, with work, movement and sound. The T.V. and radio are constantly on because we cannot bear our own company and so give ourselves no time or opportunity to know 'me'. Everyone needs the personal space to spend some time alone, so a caring family will ensure that there is adequate privacy for all. The freedom to be alone without also being lonely comes only from the security of knowing that one really belongs somewhere, that one is welcome and loved, and will not somehow miss out by withdrawing occasionally for a time. Aloneness is a creative, voluntary separation from others in order to return to them refreshed and strengthened. The church family has a special responsibility to its single members because if they do not feel sufficiently secure and nurtured they will not be able to use their times alone in any creative way, their talents will be lost or underused, and they will suffer real loneliness.

e. *Extending relationships*

A family is not only the nest which protects and nurtures the fledgelings, it must also launch them out into the wider world, encouraging its members into new avenues of service, new areas of work and witness. This is dealt with briefly in the section on responsibility within the church family (see 3e). There is often a real need to help single people make relationships outside the church as well as within it, and this is especially important for those who work in Christian organizations. They need to meet non-Christians, and to mix in wider circles. When couples entertain they generally invite other couples, but singles find it helpful when they are included and can extend their range of acquaintances.

2. Family relationships

a. *Provide continuity*

Being in a family provides continuity in life as generation succeeds generation. While growing up children are immersed in the 'now' and bring current terminology and technology into the home. Today's seven-year-old is more conversant with computers and their language than relatives in their seventies are likely to be, and information on matters like metrication comes more easily from the child now growing up with it. As children become adult most will marry and the subsequent children will in turn become a new focus of interest and source of information on contemporary issues throughout the wider family. Older people contribute their wisdom, stability and sense of history to balance the uninformed enthusiasm and immediacy of youth. Single people are often cut off from the education and balance provided by other generations.

b. *Wide variety*

The church family provides all members with the opportunity to forge relationships with a wide variety of people of both sexes, all ages, many different occupations, and having diverse interests. This rich variety of outlook and age is a great stimulus, hopefully preventing single people from becoming too narrow and confined in attitude. The stimulation of having close contact with many others should extend individuals, helping each one to develop all his talents and gifts.

c. *Rubbing off corners*

The tempests within the security of family also act as very necessary sandpaper, rubbing off the rough edges that all unfinished products have. We are his workmanship, but not yet perfected. Part of the finishing process is the continual rubbing along with other imperfect people. Single people (especially those living alone) particularly need those who love them enough to risk a rebuff when they point out personal quirks, endeavouring to check the excesses and imbalances that can develop insidiously. Correction and confrontation are necessary at times but will not be undertaken by, nor accepted from, strangers. Single people in particular tend to associate with those whose characters complement their own, but also need those who are prepared to contradict. To be constructive, this needs to be contained within a nurturing, caring, family atmosphere.

d. *Enable interaction*

True family relationships will only develop when individuals really meet and get to know each other. They do not evolve when people merely attend meetings together. The church must therefore be a place where people interact with each other, learning to exchange more than comments on the weather or criticism of the services. Many churches serve coffee after worship, encouraging folk to mingle and meet each other. Some have meals together, a regular parish breakfast or evening meal before the monthly prayer meeting as well as on special occasions; breakfast following the Easter sunrise service, tea to welcome missionaries on furlough and harvest supper. This may be a feast, or a deliberately austere meal in memory of those countries stricken by drought, flood, famine, or earthquake.

Getting to know and care for one another means meeting on other occasions and in smaller numbers than gather for Sunday worship or special occasions. Groups from particular neighbourhoods meeting regularly in each other's houses are helpful, especially if there is a fair mix of resources and age groups, of marrieds and singles, and the meetings are not confined to a traditional format of prayer and bible study only, but use a variety of ways to encourage members in sharing themselves, not just their thoughts, with each other.

e. Foster spontaneity

Some of the best family times are the ones that just happen, the spontaneous celebration or get together for the sheer enjoyment of each other's company.

Following evening service at a friend's church, I overheard a young husband, after ascertaining his wife hadn't planned anything for supper, enthusiastically saying, 'Let's go down to the pub then', and gathering a few others they all went off for an impromptu meal. A suddenly arranged summer evening picnic in the local park, or someone's back yard, or novices having a go at boating on the lake, give all the more enjoyment when they are unexpected.

As a church family we must learn to spend time being with people where they happen to be just because we want to be with them, and not for any other reason than that they are important. It is not the work they are doing, or the thing we want to ask of them, but they themselves that are important. This means we will stop and chat with them where they are—on the door-step or out in the allotment, down at the disco or queueing at the chippie. Too often we nod and hurry by, intent on important work for God, forgetting that people matter more than most meetings.

3. Responsibility within the church family

a. Mutual support

Mutual responsibility is a feature of normal family life. When there's a minor job to be done, a button to be sewn on or a torn article mended in a hurry, there is usually help at hand. If there's a decision to be made there are people with whom to talk over the pros and cons in passing, to consider the possibilities and alternatives without making a special issue of the matter. A single person living alone either has to make his own decisions without such informal discussion, or consider the subject important enough to introduce as a definite item at the next meeting. If the housegroup is really being family and is genuinely concerned for everyday matters like these, then practical help should come almost as naturally—a neighbour dropping in to mend a fuse (better still, showing how it is done) or to chat things over.

b. Sharing decisions

Sharing the process of making decisions in everyday matters as well as major ones, by informal discussion, and by prayer, is an important way of sharing in one another's lives as family members. Because we belong to one another any decision, however small, is important to and affects the whole group. Each person in the housegroup contributes this knowledge and skill, whether in domestic tasks or some other area like applying for government grants, filling in insurance forms or whatever it may be.

c. Helping one another

Noticing a need and offering help on specific occasions is more valuable than vaguely saying 'do tell me if there's every anything I can do'. However well meant that may be many people, and especially singles, find it hard to ask. Often they also find it hard to accept help even when sincerely offered for a particular task, but are more likely to be able to accept if their assistance has been sought at other times, and if helping one another is an accepted and expected pattern of life.

Giving and receiving help needs sensitivity on the part of the giver, not to encroach on another's privacy, and grace on the part of the recipient to be able to accept thankfully. When someone is busy and preoccupied (as when nursing a sick relative) it may be a gerat help when a neighbour brings in a casserole or a freshly baked cake, and a relief when another offers to mow the lawn or weed the garden (provided he knows which are the weeds!) as long as this springs from a genuine concern and does not in any way imply inefficiency or the inability to cope.

Helping one another can, and should, be fun. Fellowship is likely to be deepened and extended during a weekend spent helping to decorate a member's house or in some other project of mutual benefit.

d. Making allowances

Time itself is a factor that often leads to misunderstanding. It is true that singles have fewer commitments in one respect, no children to ferry back and forth to clubs, music or sport, but they do have all the other chores of daily life to manage alone. Shopping, cooking, cleaning and general maintenance, all correspondence and arrangements have to be done by one instead of two. It is easy for singles to think that couples have more help than they actually do from each other, and for marrieds to assume that singles have more time available to them, when in fact we all need to make allowances for each other.

e. In the community

Members of the church family are not only responsible for one another's welfare, but also for encouraging each other to take some responsibility in the community where they live and the places where they work. Interested members with the right aptitudes should be encouraged to participate in local activities, to serve on committees or work's councils if asked, and to be involved more actively in local politics.

When they do these things, their service must be recognized as a Christian responsibility. The time and energy involved must be taken into account when considering whether to ask them to take on further church activities, and they should receive the prayer support of the church; they need it in order to be light and salt in dark and often unwholesome places.

f. Special occasions

Traditional family times like Christmas and other Bank Holidays, annual holidays, birthdays and other especially personal occasions can be very lonely for singles. The church family needs to be sensitive and imaginative about such times. Some single people prefer to go off alone on holiday or to team up with other singles, but others only do so because they never have the chance to accompany and contribute to a family group or a gathering of several families. There are other less joyful occasions when single people can be terribly isolated and alone, most especially at funerals and times of serious illness or other anxiety when a friend's offer of company, and of accompanying to the hospital, can be a real life-line.

g. *Times of stress*

There is need for increased care and support at times of extra stress like changing jobs or taking on new responsibility, whether this be buying a first house or assuming the care of elderly relatives. The need for help from others lessens in every situation except the last. The single person here has to take on a task that will become more exacting as time passes, demanding more physically, emotionally, and perhaps financially. When death occurs the single person has to cope with all the immediate practical matters of funeral and other arrangements as well as legal and financial affairs that may drag on for months or even years, in addition to facing their own loss and rebuilding a life for themselves again. At times like these church members can indeed be family, guiding and helping in the often complex practical problems and providing the emotional support needed to make the necessary personal adjustments.

h. *Changing life style*

A change of life style often follows a bereavement, or other crisis, but may also be desirable, especially for single people, at other times. What is right for any individual at one stage of his development may not remain so for ever and the church family may need to show responsibility for one another by encouraging and facilitating alternative patterns of living.

Those who have lived very much alone and to themselves may need help to begin sharing part of their lives with others, and some may benefit from sharing their home with another. There are many patterns from which to choose, from having lodgers (short or long term) to sharing with one or more others on an equal basis, or even becoming part of a community. Christian communities vary in size from one nuclear family with one or more unrelated single adults to many large households some composed of families and singles while others are all singles. There are also communities of commitment where families and singles live in their own homes but share major household items, events and decisions, and become much more a part of each other's lives than in many a natural family or geographical community. Anyone, and especially a single person, needs the combined wisdom, natural and spiritual, of fellow church members 'being family', before embarking on any such major change.

i. *Recognizing gifts*

A further way in which members show responsibility for one another is in recognizing each other's gifts, encouraging their development, providing opportunities for their use—and preventing abuse. When there is a close sharing contact throughout the week, abilities and gifts, both natural and spiritual, will become apparent in individuals. Equally important, the non-possession of other ones will also be evident, and these facts should be shared as in any family. Then there is the matter of leadership, Too often church activities are led by either couples or singles, but often there would be great benefit all round if leadership could be shared by a couple and a single person working equally together.

4. Recreation in the church family

Looking at the natural order in creation, life ought to be a balance between activity and rest, work and play, solitude and company—and, for humans, one must add assessing facts and using imagination. Recreation to aid the re-creation of the person can include any, or all, of these and certainly it should be used towards achieving a style of life that is as balanced as possible overall. Just three areas will be looked at here.

a. Creativity

Churches need to pay more positive attention to the creative aspect of recreation if they are going to cater for the whole person. The regular programme should provide opportunity for members to explore and develop their natural abilities in as wide an area as possible, utilizing the known skills of some to draw out hidden talent in others. One church held a series of creative workshops, beginning with music, dance and drama then extending to include art, craft and writing groups meeting simultaneously. They met both to enjoy and develop their individual gifts, and to blend them together to enhance the Sunday worship from time to time. Another church has held an occasional members' hobbies exhibition, displaying a variety of hitherto unknown activities. These included dinghy building; wool gathering, spinning and weaving; glass blowing; models made in a great variety of materials and size; different types of photography and cinefilms; intricate sewing from wedding gowns to minute embroidery; unusual knitted items; many toys; a great diversity of drawing, painting, carving, etching and allied arts. The breadth and scope was amazing, stimulating those who took part and all who came to look around. Most of this work was done outside church circles; at adult education classes, school, home and college and the fact that it was exhibited in a church brought many outsiders in to look around. Not only producing the articles and hobbies displayed but staging them on this special occasion helped people to get to know each other, singles and marrieds meeting and mixing together in a natural way, around a common interest.

b. Fun

Some churches organize various sports (football, badminton, sailing, cycling) for those so inclined, often playing with or against other churches and organizations, but more could be done for the less athletic. Informal indoor games afternoons have proved popular with one church, board and card games from Cluedo to Happy Families, jigsaws and other puzzles, Mahjong, Mastermind and whatever else is popular at the time being available at different tables at one end of the hall, with skittles, quoits and table-tennis at the other for the more energetic. People are free to come and go, moving from one activity to another, just glad to be with each other.

Whatever our church programme, we must allow for and encourage spontaneous initiative in doing things together on the spur of the moment, an impromptu supper at the local chippie or take-away, though other fun activities do take varying degrees of pre-planning. Bank Holiday rambles, outings to places of interest, indoors and out, theatre and concert parties, talent evenings and progressive suppers in which each course is prepared and eaten in a different home, perhaps ending up with coffee and communion, have all helped to build up real relationships. Weekends away together, longer holidays in a hotel, out camping or, more ambitiously, to Israel, can all be arranged by a church or group of churches and will help singles of all ages to integrate better with each other and with families.

c. Let's have a change

What is work to one person can be truly recreational (though not necessarily restful) to another. Some single people are pleased at the opportunity